How to use this book

Follow the advice, in italics, given for you on each page.
Support the children as they read the text that is shaded in cream.
***Praise** the children at every step!*

Detailed guidance is provided in the Read Write Inc. Phonics Handbook

9 reading activities

Children:

Practise reading the speed sounds.

Read the green, red and challenge words for the story.

Listen as you read the introduction.

Discuss the vocabulary check with you.

Read the story.

Re-read the story and discuss the 'questions to talk about'.

Read the story with fluency and expression.

Answer the questions to 'read and answer'.

Practise reading the speed words.

Speed sounds

Consonants *Say the pure sounds (do not add 'uh').*

f ff	l ll le	m mm **(mb)**	n nn kn	r rr	s ss **(se)** ce	v ve	z zz s	sh	th	ng nk

b bb	c k ck ch	d dd	g gg	h	j	p pp	qu	t tt	w wh	x	y	ch tch

Vowels *Say the sounds in and out of order.*

at	hen head	in	on	up	day	see happy he	high find	blow no

zoo	look	car	for door snore	fair	whirl	shout	boy spoil

Each box contains one sound but sometimes more than one grapheme. Focus graphemes are ***circled****.*

Green words

Read in Fred Talk (pure sounds).

blow girl live house for stool poor hard

oil spoil soil join coin joint boy joy toy lamb

Read in syllables.

yell\`ow	→	yellow	a\`round	→	around
be\`tween	→	between	may\`be	→	maybe
des\`troy	→	destroy	en\`joy	→	enjoy
a\`ppoint	→	appoint	roy\`al	→	royal
em\`broid\`er	→	embroider	oy\`ster	→	oyster

Read the root word first and then with the ending.

live	→	lived	toil	→	toiled	boil	→	boiled
hoist	→	hoisted	employ	→	employed	point	→	pointed
present	→	presented						

Red words

through once here son there who your her

Challenge words

scented

The jar of oil

Introduction

What would you buy or do if your family won the lottery?
How would it change your life?
Do you think you'd be happier? Why?

A rich prince gives a poor man a jar of scented oil. The poor man starts to dream about selling the oil for gold coins. He dreams of what he would do with the money. But, because of the man's foolishness, something goes wrong.

Story written by Gill Munton
Illustrated by Tim Archbold

Vocabulary check

Discuss the meaning (as used in the story) after the children have read each word.

	definition:	sentence/phrase:
toiled	*worked*	*He had toiled so hard.*
scented	*sweet smelling*	*The prince gave him a gift of scented oil.*
hoisted	*lifted*	*He hoisted the jar of oil onto his back.*
a wooden cot	*a simple bed*	*He had a wooden cot in his room.*
embroidered	*decorated material with sewing thread*	*My princess will have the best embroidered dresses.*
soil	*earth*	*The oil was sinking into the soft soil by the door.*
destroyed	*ruined, lost, gone*	*He had destroyed the jar of oil.*

Punctuation to note in this story:

1. Capital letters to start sentences and full stop to end sentences

2. Capital letters for names

3. Exclamation marks to show anger, shock and surprise

The jar of oil

Once there lived a poor man who was employed to do odd jobs for a prince.

One day, he had toiled so hard in the royal gardens that the prince presented him with a gift – a big jar of scented oil.

"Thank you, Your Royal Highness," said the poor man.

He hoisted the jar of oil on to his back and took it to his little house. He had just one room, with a three-legged stool, a wooden cot and a shelf for his food.

He put the jar of oil on the shelf.

"I will sell it," he said to his yellow dog, pointing at the jar of oil with his stick.

"I will sell it for a jar of gold coins.
Think of all the good food I can enjoy when I am a rich man. Oysters, boiled goose, and big joints of lamb.
Hot bread fresh from the grill.
Sweet milk puddings, and banana jelly.

I will ask a rich girl - maybe a princess - to join me. We will marry, and live in a grand house - maybe a palace - with soft carpets and bright woollen rugs.

My princess will have the best embroidered dresses, with splendid rings on her fingers and gold around her neck.

Our garden will be full of green plants and tall trees. I will grow lemons, and mangos. And I will appoint a poor man, to do all the odd jobs.

We will have a strong, handsome son. His hair will be as black as midnight, and his lips as red as a sunset. He will sleep between cool satin sheets in a carved bed, with the softest pillows.

This boy will have lots of books and toys, but I will not spoil him. He will be as good as gold, and will bring us much joy.

We will play together as dad and son. We will play fight with pointed swords and sticks like this! Oi! Oi!

And he swished his stick through the air, crashing it on to the floor.

But he had knocked the jar of oil off the shelf!

The jar was smashed to bits. As for the oil, it ran right across the floor and out of the house, sinking into the soft soil by the door.

A poor man - and a foolish one. With one blow, he had destroyed the jar of oil - and all his grand plans as well.

Questions to talk about

Re-read the page. Read the question to the children. Tell them whether it is a **FIND IT** *question or* **PROVE IT** *question.*

FIND IT

- ✓ *Turn to the page*
- ✓ *Read the question*
- ✓ *Find the answer*

PROVE IT

- ✓ *Turn to the page*
- ✓ *Read the question*
- ✓ *Find your evidence*
- ✓ *Explain why*

Page 9:	FIND IT	*Why did the prince give the poor man the jar of oil?*
Page 10:	PROVE IT	*How can we tell that the man is poor from the description of his house?*
Page 11:	FIND IT	*What does the man plan to do with the oil?*
Page 12:	FIND IT	*What will the princess wear?*
Page 13:	PROVE IT	*What does the man imagine his son will be like?*
Page 14:	PROVE IT	*What happens when the man swishes his stick around?*
Page 15:	PROVE IT	*What happened to the man's grand plans when he knocked over the oil?*

Questions to read and answer

(Children complete without your help.)

1. Why did the prince let the old man have the oil?

2. What did the old man want to get with the gold coins?

3. What will he grow in his garden?

4. What will his son have?

5. Why is the old man foolish?

Speed words

Children practise reading the words across the rows, down the columns and in and out of order clearly and quickly.

between	garden	lived	around	marry
house	boy	toys	enjoy	boiled
pointing	coins	through	over	called
who	find	other	now	their